WILD HEART

STINE JOY

WILD HEART

POEMS

WILD HEART

Copyright © Stine I Joy Jorgensen 2012

ISBN 978-0-9571195-0-5

www.StineJoy.com

Published April 2012 by The Bald Truth of Motion International Ltd
Registered in England Company Number 05403004
2 Mountbatten Close, Weymouth Dorset, DT4 9ET,
United Kingdom
Email: info@stinejoy.com
Phone: 07411588281

Printed and distributed by Lightning Source UK Ltd.
Registered in England and Wales Company number 4042196
Registered office 5 New Street Square, London, EC4A 3TW

Cover Photographer: Mia Elisabeth Nielsen
Stylist/Make-up-Artist: Rikke Josephine Winther

FOR SAVANNAH JOY

CONTENTS

BRAVE LOVE

"The least of things with a meaning is worth more in life than the greatest of things without it.

- Carl Jung.

"Your task is not to seek for love, but merely to seek and find all the barriers within yourself that you have built against it."   - Rumi

PREFACE

"Poetry is not a luxury. It is a vital necessity of our existence. It forms the quality of light within which we can predicate our hopes and dreams toward survival and change, first made into language, then into idea, then into more tangible action. Poetry is the way we help give name to the nameless so it can be thought. The farthest horizons of our hopes and fears are cobbled by our poems, carved from the rock experiences of our daily lives." Audre Lorde (1934-1992)

For me, poetry has always been centered in truth; it is the voice of the unfiltered and raw quintessence of life. It's an exploration of what we are about - a revelation of the thin margins between heart and thought. Words that help us to feel and deepen our understanding of ourselves, whether it is through the expression of the intricacies of nature, the wonder of our existence, or the pathways to love.

I am endlessly fascinated with human emotion; our ability to experience the grace of vulnerability and humility in love and at the same time contain such insoluble strength and faith. I write poetry to stir my own and others' spirits, to push my own boundaries to grow as well as taking the passage to openheartedness in life and love. We are all the refinement of a soul through time, and the more we are willing to be intimate with ourselves and understand our paths, and who we have been, we can decide who we will become. Poetry truly has the power to connect us and open our hearts to the magnificence of the world we live in. Like great song lyrics,

1

poetry can challenge and free our dispositions and almost instantly bring balance to our life experience. We are enthused to break through the paralysis of fear, so we can redefine ourselves, feel our true intuition, and unfold a vision for our lives.

Like everyone else, I am a human in training, and as one grows up and attempts to navigate through the endless opportunities and decisions we are faced with, it becomes more crucial to listen to our instincts and to follow our own hearts. In this constant noise that is such an inseparable part of life, it is our responsibility to filter what happens to us from the reality of who we are. Still, many realities exist simultaneously – we wake up every morning with the choice to be joyous or to be depressed. It is always our choice, because between every deep fear and our most illuminating desire always rests the opportunity to live with bravery and to face our own insecurities and the uncertainties life brings. There is no doubt that what we focus on, and what we feed our mind and soul with - we will become.

THE PATH

WILD HEART

Every morning
I open my eyes and
uncover
my dreams entirely.

It was what I was born for
living and loving
with half my soul resident on today's soil,
and half my soul floating in the winds of hope.

The day of the inspired, the bright morning textures,
taking shape to make signs for our dusty hearts,
in this earthly space
where most things appear to get stuck on repeat,
and behind us recollections of our cloudy past close in.

We cannot go on living like crystals in the rock,
imprisoned, vibrating, glowing in the dark,
strong yet fragile in the stillness of earth,
enduring and existing yet yearning for light.

So, uncover your dreams,
walk along unguardedly, breathing with the wind,
toward the naked mind and luminous love,
toward the natural desires

that make up your wild heart.

PROMISED DREAM

Heart is the open wind that flows and creates
governing the ocean of truth, beneath the waves.

Your heart's longings are the seeds of your reality,
yet secrets moving within cannot live by standing still.

Emotive dreams are prophecy ideals,
pregnant beginnings that one day shall be:

So the flower waits in its bud,
and the child in its womb.

For the highest vision of the spirit
is to realize its burning truth.

The transcendent is found in the inspired,
for it owns the reality of its promised dream.

CLENCHED FISTS

All day it stormed, imposing control
my clenched fists resisted the wind's haul.
Suddenly, a gale rolled out my destiny
with its neatly folded dreams.
Gushes travelled through my shadows
abruptly slamming their door,
then a ferocious whirlwind stirred all doubts.
My heart surrendered in the midst of it all.

WHO WILL?

In the nothingness of time
we live, crossing its bridges, from dream - to survive.
The roots get set, weathered by storm,
compromised, whimpering, out of sight.

With naked hands we compose each day
as the petals of today, yesterday, and tomorrow fly by,
but in our hearts, the high tide is filled with hope,
like a seed we must rise, only we have forgotten how.

The sun opens our tightened fists
as we swim the deep waters of our mistaken fate.
Who will, who won't, who sleeps, who wakes?

We behold no never, for the earth's hub is burning
this flame, that flutters in each heart.
We cannot give up, not without trying,
Thus let the feet, the hands, the heart,
walk their destined path.

Humans in Training

We are all humans in training
making sense of life, as we walk along
its delicate thread of time,
living in the art form of continuous aspiration,

unfolding what we are about to become.
We run towards the flame
pockets filled with dreams
and a heart as wild as the untamed;

thump

thump

thump

thump

Somehow we lose our way, it seems,
lose sight of what moved us
during the simpler times, so busy
carrying our loads, so little time to love.

Still, the sun was meant to outshine the dark,
empty eyes are hungry for a new start,
flowers are willing to open,
reveal everything they've got; bloom,

let go and simply trust.

MELODY OF THE HEART

There is no failure or answer, no correct choice.
Still, your mind keeps on wandering
through notes of thoughts and stories.
Mountains contain as much depth as stature,
every seed holds its perfect plan,
inside the wind, there are infinite storms
and somewhere in all of life's blessings
you belong.

Take part in the daily toils and walk the path
that leaves you inspired,
but don't be of them:
Be true to the melody
that captivated you as a child,
the flowers that held your dreams,
and the spring that overflew your heart.
This melody is playing, still.

EVERY NEW DAY

Every new day
my eyes
recreate the world
in the reflection
of the blazing sun.

Old stories,
a life once lived
appear like paintings
in a black lagoon
framed by summer lilies.

Islands of memories
    floating lavishly inside my mind.

My vision alights the present
of stories yet to be told,
moments yet to be lived,
and somewhere deeply within
gratitude rings, sifting my thoughts

unfolding the simple truths:
Every new day is its own;
A prayer of manifestation,
an exact expression
of what my eyes want to be told.

In the Fusion We Exist

There, where the ocean sways into the endless skies,
the clear yellow waves burn upward like a field on fire,
and the morning sun tears off the last cluster of clouds,
to find its place, dazzling in darkness, unattached.

Let us worship this life that transcends its own purpose.
Alluring rays whose perpetual existence weaves into the earth,
and illuminates - conceives life - permanently:
Floating sea, tender wind, invincible earth.

Because, in the fusion of these textures, we exist.
You and I, waves of the sea, rising and collapsing
with the wild tenderness of the wind, and like the sun,
our inexplicable value blazes over the hills.

ESSENCE

Essence; not a dispensable
ingredient, a crucial element,
concentration, or substance
that's unique in each of us.
A pure entity that radiates
through our core, in a person
whom you've never met
but whose touch of generosity
can be felt; scent of your lover
that melts into desire, tear of sensitivity
glazed upon the eye of a powerful man,
an extract of life
that makes it worth living,
an abundance of unique quality
we can each contribute to humanity.
The most important ingredient.
Not anything or every thing!
It's in the man who stands strong
in the midst of flakes,
within the purity of a mother's
unsurpassed love for her child.
A concentration of everything
that is centered in us all.

I OWN NO MAP

I own no map
but as for longing,
I'm pretty familiar,

for a heavenly cocoon
filled with delicacies of life:
Spontaneity, passion and
petal heaped nights.

A somewhere,
one place or another
where I can live, wholly
undone with joy.

Like in the stillness
around a slumbering mind
that cannot be reached
lavishly surrendered each night.

A Wind place floating
           through a hole in the map

into the wild, imagination
seeding everything.
For each meadow with its untamed flora
is a dream envisioned and turned to light.

HANDS

Hands are the saviours of our world,
for hands cannot let ideals weaken or die.
They are the master creators that mould and make
bringing innermost dreams to live:
Fingers writing, navigating, caressing
sculpting, holding, interlocking, moulding,
learning.
Never do they seize delivering,
hands.

Hands can put guns to rest,
agree to settle disputes,
write laws on human rights,
heal wounds
and say; I love you.

The actions of our hands hold a promise,
of how our world shall at last be built.

Thus, cherish the beauty that forms in your hands,
the visions and dreams that drape your mind,
for out of them shall grow a divine world.

MY TIME

Throughout my life, the world has filled me
with acceptance and humility, yet,
beyond who I am, still, I believe I am more.
Does that make it right for Jante's law to break me
or should I obediently bend?

My heart is filled with hopeful corners,
as I tie dignity and pride to my side,
and I take chances to roil, risk, dance, and leap
into an even more fulfilling life.

The top is as ever mounded with hopefuls,
I can hear their hearts cry out, longing to feel alive
rather than compromised and stuck on survival.

As I learn to see the beauty in everything I am,
no longer – not a second – will I allow doubt
to keep my time; I know, that with nurture and purity
I will rise, because it is my time.

Note*

THE HEART OF HUMANITY

What bites the heart of humanity?
It is spoken in the universe
of our hopes and divided lives:

Two worlds of joy and despair
are waiting for us to join in their living;
gain the magnificence of a new day
or the burden of its sorrows.

If you are uneasy riding your chosen waves,
don't drag yourself along them,
get out of your thorns
rather than weep, bleed or moan them.

Let your heart fall through the hole of life
and travel only on the wide roads of love
where boundless joy and laughter
can exhaust themselves in your heart.

Hope sprouts through the earth
taking up the rhythms of life anew.
So stay open,
even if every opportunity seems closed,

Riches you cannot envision are softly unfolding your soul.

Treasure the Storms

Whomever said life is complicated
must have never felt the depth of love.

Sometimes life lights a hidden fuse
sparking thoughts of disbelief in our own truth.

The stakes are high but with only gravity to lose
look through the drapes of earnest faith.

Treasure the storms that carry your heart
infusing new beginnings whilst erasing your painful past.

Build your world on bravery of thought
let all fall away and embrace the wilderness of love.

LIFE'S DISTINCTIONS

Within the courage of being true to oneself,
judgment can't take precedence
only to live bravely with soulful skin.
Which is the only way to love, isn't it?

This mind of wisdom and naivety,
this heart of compassion and fear,
this body of spirit and lust.
Our heaven for a while.

With all of life's distinctions,
it takes courage to stay open and true.
Therefore, I have chosen simply to trust
because like oceans, we are on a perpetual journey:

Our hearts climb and bow in waves.
Just as stone and water hold their ground,
our dream is born to rise
like a blossom from its seed

only to one day reveal;
the true magnificence of our being.

SECRETS LIE HIDDEN

Secrets lie hidden within the uncultivated mind,
and in this space of vast potential
few dare to ask a simple question
in paralyzed fear of self-realization.
So we stay like this forever and a day,
until fate comes along
to stir our spirits and free up our minds.
Thus, we surrender our fragile hearts
to life
trusting love won't tear them apart.
Like a vase holding immense vulnerability,
one strike could return them in pieces.
Still, the pieces would never cease hoping
for a new beginning or a happy ending.

WHEN

When you can stand face to face with yourself
in the midst of losing your stand,
when you can still have faith in your own
in the midst of disbelief and pain,
when you still dare to love despite a broken heart
and still dare to dream
despite your painful past.
Have faith when old paths are lost
and covered trails revealed.
When you can risk all you know
and face every triumph or tragedy
with unwavering faith and hope,
or embrace adversity when there is nothing left in you,
when you can listen to judgment and blame
and still maintain your virtue,
the old you but in shapes that endlessly renew:

That's when you know the strength in the shape of you.

THERE IS A KIND OF LOVE

There is a kind of love, we desire
our entire lives; a merging
of our spirit with another.

Thorns beg the world
to let the rose bloom,

and the shell cocoons the pearl
to keep its beauty and mystery untold.

At dawn, the sun yearns to illuminate my life.
As it pours its warmth onto my face,
I ask for it to release me,
like an overdose it shuts down my thoughts
and opens me up to feel;

life at its purest.

THIS LIFE

This life is a collision of contrasts – as if it sends beauty
out against the waves. And we – the human *race*,
we rush, run, and pace through the streets,
so we can be worthy of stillness and inner peace.

THE VERGE OF TRUTH

Here, I came to the verge of truth,
entangled in everything I had already heard.
I am walking along this stony path,
and there's nothing you can throw at me.
I live, wherever I am - blessed
like migrating birds fly
from the night rolling over
to the days that always die.

Beautiful in the rawness of the dark
I begin
listening to the world,
let it burrow an opening to my dreams,
until one moment;
a vision falls at my feet,
and a voice speaks,
already knowing who I am.
I am stunned by its accuracy
plucking the petals of rules
from the freedom beyond.

THIS FLAME

This flame, this earth the billions of feet
of every man have walked upon, ignited and burning
within us, without an ending, with no actual death,
it lives the eternal life of the natural world.

Yesterday's flare starts living under today's shadow
amongst wide open eyes and curious fingers.
So too will tomorrow's exhilaration surrender
to the inevitable river of night.

As we gaze into time, future, the faceless, death and hope,
life folds its wings over our hearts.
No one can stop the force of man's true path,
as he forms and creates alongside the trembling of time.

How many days have we lived with sleepy hearts?
How far can we walk with the load of this heavy mind?
Time knows nothing about the end, it just goes on,
like life, so we have to live it while we can.

Pay Attention

How exquisitely the autumn leaves burst into flames.
Still, they are safe up high,
until the night starts falling,
and the cold turns over our burning dreams.
So we learn to trim them down, no question,
hushing our hopes, ambitions, and reasons.
It is something we must do,
if we doubt following the path made for our own shoes,
well knowing that in silence screams the truth.
It's within ourselves we must travel to find it.
The fire may weaken, yet there is no other way.
We must find the magical in this path
and somehow shape our own fate,
decide where these seeds must be sown and nurtured,
until our dream rises anew.

THIS HUMAN DANCE

This human dance is a ballroom;
every moment compels a new step.

A tango of passion,
a ballet of longing,
a foxtrot of flow,
a rumba of sensuality,
a break-dance of control
a folk dance of trust.

Embrace and move with them all!
So when the music plays,
the footwork is forgotten.
When the emotion arrives,
the dance has already been chosen.
Since when the heart is open,
its rhythm can finally guide.

The dance is easy. Feel at ease
and you will be moved.
The true dance is to live openly
to forget the precise steps
and to move with your own beat.

MY MARK

Life is washing over my heart,
its mission is set in stone,
the roots of love pervade
from the depths of my soul.

I vow to put my mark on this earth,
walk the path that reveals my heart,
let the river carry me forth,
until I ascend with inspiration
enough to pick me up from every fall.

Since we are all searching from a need to be fulfilled,
thus pools of joy spill drops of enchantment onto the earth;
heavenly rays weaving from our hands onto earthly things,
knowing each mark has the power to elevate our world.

IN SILENCE

In silence, you are open to your whole self;
to intuition, to guidance, to your purpose
- even miracles.
The abstract movement of internal conversation
takes us to a better understanding of life.
Disengage from the television, the e-mail, the to-dos;
instead be curious, question and seek;
the answers will find you,
and the truth will wing its way into your heart.
Still, we must take the utmost care, in the questions we ask,
because the answers will be their mirror.
Paint them with precision and everything that matters most;
untamed thoughts peeling the skin to your heart.
Thus, embrace the edge of failure
and let yourself be moved, unguardedly,
since enthusiasm will rise, when your universe is open,
for spirit to spill out the meaning of your life.

PROGRESS

At night, I feel alive, because with me
my illuminating dreams sleep.
I feel them slowly intensifying
becoming real with the night's depth.
My soul fiercely invigorated
for whatever life I wake up to wear,
it will become me.
Only progress can take the lead.

IF

If you are what you have,
if you are what you do,
if you are what you attain,
you are understood
by what you cannot understand.
And if you don't have,
if you don't do,
if you don't attain,
you cannot be sure of anything.
So you let go of your ego's expectations,
and the old truth becomes a lie.
Until a new truth ascends,
and you are sure of nothing
and know of nothing else,
than surrendering to the purpose of your life.

BRAVE LOVE

BRAVE LOVE

A BETTER LIFE

Savage heart, naked light
of absolute transparency, of luminous dawn --:
I promise I am worthy, ready, for the time of our lives,
set to throw our souls through the fire of glory!

I have heard that dreams rise when our hearts burn.
Thus winds of change and love play a symphony in my home,
mind, and heart, blowing wild and free,
until wings of grace lift them into balance.

Just as the heavens cry to blur the line of our horizon,
the audacious noon gratifies and nourishes hope,
so I grow fonder of life's honest days.

The untamed gales of autumn lure us
with time, new paths, growth, and light
as we shatter these cracked walls to a better life.

LET LOVE BE

Let love be dishonest, scandalous and even hopeless.
The cynic will analyze its faults and judge its character,
whilst the romantic experiences love just the way it is.

THE HORIZON

The horizon floats over the world
featherlike softness
triumphantly standing on top of the earth
privately dancing for each of us.
You gently shatter
our doubts.
There, a worrying child.
There, a drug-filled night.
From your substance, we rush into life,
and its line changes with the seasons;
the warmth of sunrays, the clean chill of ice.
It is hopeful, its moods of colours,
it is forthcoming, its tilted clouds.
Its presence is filled with fireworks,
thus the night cannot roll over;
for life has just begun,
and with bravery we expose our hearts
along its jagged path.

HAVE FAITH

Have faith in the night
though it may dim your vision.

Have faith in silence
though it exposes your inner voice.

Have faith in new beginnings
though they consist only of hope.

Have faith in truth
though it is challenged by lies.

Have faith in love
though it asks you to surrender your heart.

OFFER YOUR ALL

I keep looking around.
Who has it and who doesn't?
Everyone has their prolific mounds of dreams,
yet do we have faith like the ocean

in the shell, always splitting open
revealing the invisible, listen well:
Feel how the flowers rise and open their petals;
willing to offer their all to the world.

Our bodies memorize every rise
and, more so, every fall,
and with trembling legs,
we shuffle forward into life.

Those who live in love open effortlessly;
like hands for a newborn child,
trustingly put love and courage
before the limiting mind.

THE THINGS

The things you love
      are vulnerable
not in spirit
      but in their surrender.

The things you worry about
      are imperious
not in their existence
      but in your imagination.

AS YOUNG GIRLS WE DREAM

As young girls we dream
of our hearts being ripped open
saturated with love,
swept off our feet,
and whisked away to a life
of devotional openness in love.

As women we hope that our hearts
will become the source of radiance,
that inspires our entire family
and awakens our children's deepest gifts.

As mature women we know
that our strength is the beauty
of our heart's surrender,
the radiant offering of our love.

Our love opens hearts endlessly;
our lovers', our children's, strangers'
- the heart of mankind:
Even when they otherwise forget
love's profound depth.

BEAUTY UNBOUND

Little girls
dancing in the light of the sun
like fluttering butterflies;
joy in their feet,
swing in their waist,
arms claiming the sky,
flowing with life but without form,
outshining the rays of the sun.
Soon,
mothers join in
dancing together as love.
No amount of concrete
can keep this rose beneath the ground.
So grandmothers unite the dance,
young hearts and old souls
like a flower they bloom.
Beauty unbound.

IF LOVE COULD WRAP US

If love could wrap us in its immortal flame,
it would ask us to rise above, create, and conduct

                     from the inside out.

To let the things we hide within rebirth into light,
allow nothing but trust to cling to our mind:

Until we speak only with love's voice,
       touch solely with love's hands,
              See only with love's heart,

                persistently.

Love waves its wand of magic,
its spell of entangled freedom around it,
and we turn with the motion of this sage,
so rich in life that the earth spins through the sky.

Welcome its mystery,
its waves of sorrows and joys
for each has been delivered as a gift from beyond.

MY HEART FLOATS

My heart floats from my hands into life,
as each day arrives and breaks its thumping silence.
I love to carve our emergent love kingdom
softly: intuition igniting my fingers.

Taking charge: a vision, that opens and lifts
my hands, transforming thought into living flares,
love is so utterly invisible, like the wind
just blows, nowhere to be seen,

weaving into everything like the power of a simple dream-
and now, suddenly, we bring it to life,
fingers writing, lifting, forming - tied to a purer motion,

holding and lifting pregnant thoughts, seeds
of kindness, empathy, compassion, sensitivity,
cultivating even the palest of hearts
by all joys with the rays of our hands.

THIS WONDROUS WORLD

Everyone should feel in awe
of this adventure - your life –
this wondrous world!

I am not sure for whom the news speaks--
the haters, the fearful, the faceless?
I wonder.
Do they campaign for fear, death, or the living thing?
As the earth flies by our hearts
tainted with TVs, bombs, and blood,
I notice,
upon these faces that say nothing,
there is something;
hopeful - silent yet stirring.
And have you forgotten how it feels to trust?
And have you clamoured toward you, yourself,
to rely on your own heart?
As for the world, it is sublime and strong,
mystical, mesmerizing, and captivating;
it holds us in a mix of power
and sweetness, as we keep on walking,
avoiding the distorted paths.

LOVE

As children, we existed for its presence.
A place where nothing fades,
where there are no limits
only transactions of grace.
Your heart is your messenger,
when you lose faith, or feel it expand again,
when you dread your swaying fragility.
This purity unravels your fears, love.

*

YOUR LUMINOUS WINGS

Every morning I see your brilliance clear as day.
Surely, little one, you've got enough to fill the skies.
You arrive in the rays of sun and soft wind
surrounding me with your pure embrace.
I listen for one voice above the others,
as you drown out the constant noise,
that is such an inseparable part of life.
One heart among so many hearts:
The distinguished and unassuming
peering into the mystery of life.
This seed has come to enlighten the world
with newborn serenity and surrender.
Fearlessly you leap into the whirlwind of life
leaving footprints across this bridge of my existence.
Your purpose is set in stone
like a leaf serves its tree,
the earth its roots:

You spread over the world your luminous wings.

THE LANGUAGE OF YOUR LAUGHTER

The language of your laughter;
naked words sung with blissful tone,
sliding, floating, and soaked in rhythm.

Each breath restoring the balance of my world;
its beginning spins through the wind,
echoes in my heart, drowning its lament thirst.

Its words bow like waves towards their blessing
- celebrating life's presence.
The language of your laughter,

your mouth, your light, your wit,
are all an entangled integrity of your spirit,
exhalations of intricate vibrations that weave into
the rhythms of life, holding and lifting it to the sky.

LIKE A SEED

Like a seed aching for its flower,
my womb is longing for your presence,
where ever you are.

It seems our love flies with no resting;
A nomad wandering the entire world.
Still, our embrace takes you back home,
where you belong.

Like a wild flower longs for its meadow,
in your presence, I am drawn into the light of life,
all shadows evaporated.

Sweet child of mine,
your heart is showing me my way.
Your own woman in the making
unfolding your love one petal at a time.

A flower rising with dignity and pride,
fragile, yet as powerful as a dream I once had
to assist the beginning of your life.

WHEN I AM WITH YOU

When I am with you, I hold the daylight,
enlightening the deepest memories
in my smile. Hardly touching,
I bow like a wave towards your completeness,
as if the life in our embrace
would slowly reveal what will be.

I indulge in your beauty,
moving my hand over your skin
barely able to be touched,
on the side of your face,
its brightness floating in the dark.
I am water, and you are held in my sway.

I feel your little heart beat
and find my quiet heart grown wild.
Your smile responds the way
words wish they could
making daylight break this deserted night.

OUR INNER LANDSCAPE

Did you see it?
Rays stretching in the horizon,
astonishing in their quietude.
Did you notice them?
Bowing under the gleaming meadows of rain
owning their wholesome splendour.
A prophecy reality,
with its artful sunstrokes of blossoms and trees,
mountains and lakes roiling in the bluest light of day.
The natural world offers itself to our imagination,
light and colours beaming in the darkness of despair,
moving across our inner landscape.
Valleys echo your voice, leaving all doubts behind,
the wind transforms loneliness into a shapeless thing.
Can you hear it singing your choice of freedom?
A melody carried by whistles and flutes, softly
entering and moving through your skin,
until you find your own heart, in the nature of things.

DARK AND LIGHT

Afraid to love our own darkness
we cultivate purity of being;
white sheets, faultless intellect,
pleasing them all, until our secret's revealed.
A kind boy.
A good girl.
So we were taught
to be.
They say light equals authenticity
and darkness a disloyal mind.
Still,
if love enthrones your spirit,
darkness and light become seedlings
of a passionate earth:
Our authentic selves.
Light breeds shadows
and in sweetness dwells wildness.
For, what is more enticing,
than a man who demands to take your soul?
Or a woman who dances, openly claiming you her own?
Self-control is strength
though not when it comes to love.
Because, to make love an immortal piece of art
we have to paint it with striking contrasts
and bless passion for a life fulfilled
by the effects of darkness entwined with light.

PURITY

Let your desire at night draw me in
tip over the dignity of our darkness
like sweet singing emerging from the wilds
luring us with a glimpse of the unseen.
The moon sinks dreams into the earth
like permeating shadows of the stars
that form our eyes of intuition.
Love, let's rise again, fasten our grip on life,
with hands that move and create,
upholding the world each day
and immersing – being, honestly – continually,
so that the heavens will hush themselves
to hear the purity that we are becoming

SWEET LOVE

Your touch owns my body,
and my softness flutters in your soul.
What is living in your dreams will ascend
with my wings to heaven.

In my field at sunrise you are the nourishing rays,
as your depth makes my meadow flourish,
until all is filled with light and deepened with consciousness:
We're instantly reminded how miraculously sweet love can be.

THE PLAINS OF PURE LIFE

You are the plains of pure life,
the mountain heights of faith
on a crowded earth clouded
with desert sand grains.
You are all that is strong to endure
and courageous to love.

You, are a higher round of life
leading me on secret paths,
where surface has very little part
in the reality of things.

Through you, lives begin to brighten,
with a vision passionate as fire
you ride the clouds to a new world
beyond silent dreams.

In your arms, love is in season,
shutting the doors upon old substitutes,
opening windows of least resistance
with the view of rejuvenating joys
where only soulful instruments are enjoyed.

LOVE'S WAY

Love's way is sometimes through touch
pulling its sky over us with adept flair.
Giving to receive, giving merely to give,
wrapped in one another's skin.

Love is building a mystery
with carefully laid stones
upheld or crumbled with lovers hands,
promises of forever with the tip of our toes.

Pinches of passion, thumps of lust,
clinches of tenderness, strokes of love:
In our loving embrace words cannot feel
all that our touch is able to say.

YOU

You, with your
  nomadic footprints
    walking along
      the path of my life
        singing with the wind
        and me.
Let's go, take off, run and sail
    toward the pinnacle of desire,
      break the blurry edges
        of light
          that softly whispers
            to uphold its vigour.
I am captivated by your presence.
    Since you, nothingness started moving.
    My heart turns to you,
      with forbidden words
        made sweeter by the vastness
        of air between us.
I am caught in our embrace
    of what could be:
      Our story imprinting
        a golden trace in my memory.

THIS MOMENT IN TIME

You turn to me, with eyes that peel the skin
of the day's haze; your hands are filled with sun.
Your lips sing to me with the tongue of the open sky;
guide me through the gloom and motions of life.

Striking on the horizon,
like black stones resting in the sand,
our two silhouettes entwine, your blood in mine,
arms begging us to hold on.

The sun falls on our soft shadow,
carrying us, crashing us onto the earth.
How soon the night comes,
how soon the day forgets.

This courageous, pure tenderness of love;
passionate fires burned to uphold this light,
this path, the full moon with its luminous eye
promises never to forget this moment in time.

YOUR TOUCH

Your touch this evening – with its desire –
between moonlight, sheets and feathers, the epitome of lust.
Already entwined – one heart in living doubleness
floating like water, wild like fire.

And you – painting my life with vivid colours – you shimmer,
grounded with roots of an oak, yet as subtle as wind.
Your heart wears a shape lost in me; yet I cannot contain you.
Together we indulge in the darkness of the night.

You call for us to join the brightness of the moon,
and we do, like birds we fly into the sky of mystery,
and the sky becomes our haven;
our love-universe roiling with worship.

LOVE IS THE FLAME

Love is the flame that illuminates life's core.
Yet, the merging of hearts is a liquid path

In the heart, a passionate demand,
in the hand, a guiding hint,
in the eye, darkness and light interconnect.

Truthful love has no expectations,
yet we reach for shapes we hope will fit
the delicate frame of our own mirror;
forgetting to borrow eyes from the other side.

Anything that comes with a rule attached
only survives the pattern of time,
but love is timelessly unconditional,
since the heart knows all that the mind cannot feel.

LET ME HOLD YOU

Let me hold you
weave us in shadows and soft repose.
Let time watch over the world outside our embrace,
let all reason creep beneath the roots of make-belief.
I will let you undo me,
let me rise to life in your arms, release me,
like a thornless rose sheltered by your hand.
Safely, I am letting go of control
whilst my heart learns to fulfill its open destiny.

Released

Sleepy with sand and soft embraces
stuck in our hurricane of lustful play,
like the wind, I cruise the skies yet way too high,
diving, rising, falling;
sweetly released from all I have let go.

My luminous eyes close
as the night floats its shadows through the streets,
drunk with salty kisses, softened by your presence
taking command of my soul.
As always in my wild ocean you are the last wave,
the one that travels with my heart into dreams.

Love me, oak of skin, weapon of conquest.
I was caged behind bars of gold
though blinded by darkness.
With you, my shell lies open in surrender
thirsty for the ocean of life, I am now willing to contain.

Presence of my man, I am filled with your depth,
I let my hands become stained with our love,
together in the wholesomeness of this root of faith,
growing wildly with desire, and infinite trust.

SENSUAL BODY

Sensual body, breaking the ranks of paradise,
falling to the earth and into your bare hands.
Ocean lines, soft, yet rough like an underground cave.
Break me, take me to the edge of a new day.

Naked, swimming, drifting in the seasons of you,
your chest as warm as the Grecian sun,
our breaths send me chills like an autumn storm.
Here, love flies more persistent than time.

Your voice fills my life with faith and bravery,
unslave my heart from its burrow of chores and apathy:
I lay down my chains -drop my petals- fragile as a naked seed.

I am lost in you, my heart drifts like a gypsy's restless mind.
Our fire nourishes the prospect of freedom from time
- so this sensual body surges to life.

HANDS ON LOVE

Close enough to search for ourselves in one another,
love crosses the bridges, from me to us,
as it lays its hands on our hopeful hearts,
and no one – not a soul – can get in the way of its path
as it floats, fragile and ferocious through life.

You and I entwined in the flawless blue skies,
where the dirt couldn't stain our words,
where fire could burn without losing hope,
where our hearts could live and progress.

Apart we have felt our hearts clenched in longing,
uprooted by the digger of mistrust.
Yet, the hard days dispersed in wind and waves.

Still we have our hands on love,
lifting our eyes to its face,
as we walk our hearts and souls
across its luminous rays.

ACKNOWLEDGEMENTS:

My deepest gratitude:

To my mother Susanne and grandmother Mona for being an unwavering source of unconditional love and strength.

To Rohan, for your magical love.
You inspire me to live in truth.

To Savannah, for being the greatest inspiration in my life.
Your heart is showing me my way.

To my wonderful brother and sister; Ulrik and Rikke Josephine.
To Martin, my father Ivan, sister Nanna, my grandparents Vagner, Henning and Elsebeth. To my parents-in-law Helen, Graham, Bertram and my dear friends and extended family.

To some of the most inspirational teachers and extraordinary poets, who have had a profound impact on my life: Wayne Dyer, Anthony & Sage Robbins, David Deida, Marianne Williamson/A Course in Miracles, James Allen, Rumi, Hafiz and Pablo Neruda.

Thank you to Photographer Mia Elisabeth Nielsen
and Stylist/Make-up artist Rikke Josephine Winter

To my Publisher The Bald Truth and Lightning Source.

Notes:

Quote 1
by Carl Gustav Jung from: "Modern Man in Search of a Soul," 1955.

Quote 2
by Jalal ad-Din Rumi (Persian Poet and Mystic, 1207-1273)

Page 1: Audre Lorde "Sister Outsider: essays and speeches" page 36. Published by Crossing Press, 1985.

*   "Jante's Law" (included in poem "My Time" page 16). A cultural expression used negatively to illustrate an attitude towards individuality and success in Scandinavia.
"The ten rules state:
1.   Don't think you're anything special.
2.   Don't think you're as good as us.
3.   Don't think you're smarter than us.
4.   Don't convince yourself that you're better than us.
5.   Don't think you know more than us.
6.   Don't think you are more important than us.
7.   Don't think you are good at anything.
8.   Don't laugh at us.
9.   Don't think anyone cares about you.
10.   Don't think you can teach us anything."
From Aksel Sandermose's Novel "A Fugitive Crosses his Tracks", 1933.

*   Poem "Love" page 46 is a remembrance and tribute to Rumi's poem about love's essence.

ABOUT THE POET:

Stine Joy was born on the 21st of July 1979 in Nykobing, Denmark. During her Childhood and as a young woman, Stine traveled extensively. She lived briefly in South America, Greece, settled in Spain for a year and later on she made her home in England with her fiancé Rohan Weerasinghe and their daughter Savannah.

Stine studied various subjects such as Linguistics, Art and Design, Social Anthropology, Photography and Human Needs Psychology at seminar and university level. These diverse studies became the foundation for her innate passion to combine her creative gifts and early love of poetry with her ever growing insight into emotional, social and spiritual development. Joy's first collection of poetry "Wild Heart" immerses into the desire to live bravely and to love without bounds.

At the time of this publication Stine Joy and her family reside in Barcelona, Spain, where she focuses on writing, painting and illustrating.

Visit the poet online at www.stinejoy.com.